Love's Sacred Vow

Beats Of Love Played in Poetry

SANJAY JOSHI

India | USA | UK

Made with ❤ on the BookLeaf Publishing Platform
www.bookleafpub.in
www.bookleafpub.com

Dedication

To all hearts that beat in love....

Preface

Welcome to my collection of love poems. Within these pages, you'll find memories of tender moments, secret whispers, and heartfelt emotions. Whether you're curled up in your favorite chair with coffee or relaxing with wine, I invite you to join me on this journey. May these verses speak to your own experiences of love and touch your heart as you read them.

Acknowledgements

To the ones who loves me completely, just as I am

1. The Reveal

Through the busy streets and city sound
A beauty appeared, just looking around

Her face was bright like the moon at night
Like perfect painting of pure delight

Her lips were red like cherry wine
Just one sweet kiss would make life fine

Her eyes were dark with golden specks
Their beauty left me weak at legs

Her hair danced wild and free all day
Like waves that never go away

Her voice was music to my ears
A tune I'll treasure through the years

Her heart shone bright with endless love
Wild as storms in skies above

As destiny's pages began to unfold
Through summer's warm breeze and winter's cold
Will she ever be mine in arms to hold

2. Heart's Flare

Like gentle rain upon the earth,
In his heart, she sparked new birth.
Each day that passed without her near,
Made his longing grow more clear.

Her serious face kept him at bay,
Too nervous even words to say.
Time drifted like leaves in fall,
While hope grew dim with friendship's call.

Then fortune smiled from stars above,
As conversation bloomed to love.
Their chats now flowed like morning light,
Making every moment of day seem bright.

Over tea they shared their days,
Two hearts wild in love's sweet haze.
Their laughter rang both pure and true,
Whether alone or in a crew.

Together they were whole and free,
Perfect as two drops in the sea.
No other soul did they require,
Their hearts ablaze with passion's fire.

Like stories old of fated love,
Two souls reunited by stars above.
A tale of hearts that were meant to meet,
Making both their lives complete.

3. First Blossom

Moments they spend together in love
Was it a dream or blessing from above

Her eyes twinkled to see him like stars
His heart skipped beats to embrace her in arms

The touch of her hand on him was so divine
He felt the moment with shiver running down his spine

They completed each other like day and night
Their skin tattooed with marks of love bite

They hold each other with affection close and tight
Vows spelled to not let each other go in moments of fight

Love was flowing like rivers, never still or staid
Between them a dance of hearts, where growth is ever-
made

Together they promised to journey distant far,

Like guiding beacons, star by star

With hearts entwined in sacred dance
Their souls ignite with love's bright lance

4. Tempting Dreams

By the glass window, a romantic embrace,
A bed adorned with wine, a dreamy space.

Soft, feathered sheets and blankets entwined,
They tasted each other's skin, lost in time.

City lights twinkled like fireflies' flight,
Slowly he kissed her, a delicate rite.

His lips traced her curves, valleys so deep,
Pausing at places where shivers would leap.

In the heart of the night, where shadows creep,
Love blossomed, forbidden and steep.

Their hearts intertwined, a daring affair,
In the cloak of darkness, they found solace rare.

Like moonlight that glimmers on leaves in the breeze,
Their passion ignited, as wild as they please.

In whispers of secrets that echo the night,
Two souls intertwine, their hearts shining bright.

5. Ocean Of Love

As the sunlight falls upon the sand,
Two lovers stroll along, hand in hand.

Each wave rolls in with foamy white,
Their feet now wet, their hearts so lite.

The salty breeze tell stories so old,
While seagulls soar through skies above.

Their laughter rings across the shore,
Two hearts at peace, asking no more.

Their footprints mark the sandy way,
Creating memories of this day.

Though tides may wash their tracks from view,
These moments shared will stay so true.

They chase the waves with childlike glee,
On shores that stretch indefinitely.

This afternoon of pure delight,
Where ocean's song makes all feel right.

Through scattered shells and glittering spray,
Where horizon bends so far away.

Their hearts beat free in love's sweet dance,
Lost in this seaside sweet romance.

In amber glow they pause to rest,
This peaceful moment, nature's best.

Their love runs deep as ocean blue,
Two souls entwined, forever true.

6. Love's Sacred Vow

I walk slowly on this path anew
To earn your trust, for love thats divine and true

Like dawn's first light, I'll softly greet your gaze
And let my heart unfold through all the days

Each whispered word a promise etched in air
No secrets held, for all my thoughts I'll share

My eyes reflect the beauty I see in your soul
A love so pure, it makes my spirit whole

If doubts should rise, like shadows in the night
I'll banish them with love's enduring light

For in your gaze, I find a sacred space
Where trust can flourish, and love finds its grace

With every touch, a vow both calm and clear
To nurture bonds where hearts can draw near

Let time reveal the depths of what we seek
A love so strong that whispers when we speak

So let me show, with every dawn's embrace
That in my heart, your trust will find its place

With hand in hand, together we will tread
And build a love where hope and dreams are spread

7. Threads Of Trust

I see you crying, face so sad,
Seeing this my heart feels bad.

My words were mean and hurt you deep,
Now all your broken trust I'll keep.

I'm sorry that I caused you pain,
Let me help you smile again.

I promise as I hold you near,
To wipe away each falling tear.

Just like the sun that brings the light,
I'll help to make your world feel right.

With loving words and gentle ways,
I'll stay beside you all my days.

When you smile, my world gets bright,
Like sunshine after darkest night.

Looking in your eyes, I know
Our love will only stronger grow

8. Hidden Yearnings

A love I find, too deep to name
An endless dance, a flickering flame

My heart, a vessel, brims with emotion
A tide of feelings, a ceaseless ocean

Like summer's breeze that whispers low
It sweeps through trees, a gentle flow

It brings a calm that wraps me tight
A soothing warmth in soft twilight

It fills my soul with purest delight
Awakens me, a star in flight

In silent awe, I find my peace
For in this love, my worries cease

The perfect love that lets me soar
Where I can be myself, and more

Your laughter sparkles, a radiant glow
A melody where my heart will grow

Your love, a hug, both warm and bright
Fills me with grace, a joyous light

With kindness shining from your heart
You weave a spell, a work of art

Like rivers flowing, never to wane
Your love, a song, a sweet refrain

A guiding star that lights my way
In your embrace, I long to stay

9. Canvas Of Her Charm

As sun sets over tall concrete and shadows play
A vision blooms, a bright bouquet

Her eyes, like gems, with secrets gleam
Sparkling pools of a sultry dream

A vibrant aura, sweet and bold
Like summer sun, a warmth untold

Her laughter rings, a siren's call
With every note, my senses fall

Curves that sway, a whispered sigh
A gentle back, flowing like wind in blue sky

Her perfect hips, a soft cascade
In every glance, my heart betrayed

Skin, a rose in morning's dew
Fragrant essence, pure and true

Lips like wine, so rich and fine
A taste of heaven, so divine

Sun-kissed dots on porcelain skin
A charming dance, where stories begin

And beauty marks, like gems bestowed
Each one a temptation, a sweet abode

Her bossom an indefinite land of snow
Red roses from them peeping through

Smooth as silk, soft as cloud, tender beneath
Rising and falling like waves with every breath

In her embrace, the world dissolves
Desire stirs, my heart resolves

A beautiful girl with a radiant glow
In her warm presence, love's fire flows

10. Gossips Over Tea

In a cozy cafe, soft lights glow,
Two souls meet, letting their love flow.

Steaming cups of chai, warm and sweet,
Sharing laughter, where heart skips a beat.

The scent of samosas fills the air,
As they sit close, lost in a stare.

Biryani spices dance on their tongues,
In this little haven, love's song is sung.

Fingers touch softly, a gentle caress,
With each bite of food, their hearts feel blessed.

"Tell me more about your day," one softly asks,
While enjoying kulcha, as love slowly basks.

At a food joint filled with flavor and cheer,
Each dish shared brings the world near.

From dosa to sweet gulab jamun,
Every tasty moment feels like a deep boon.

Together they laugh, through joy and through strife,
Creating sweet memories, like flavors in life.

In every meal shared, their bond only grows,
A love that's rich, like the curry that flows.

As they sip on chai, with eyes all aglow,
They treasure these moments, letting love show.

In this bustling world, they've found their spot,
Two souls making memories, loving a lot.

11. Lens To The Heart

In the evening light, her eyes brightly gleam,
Two pools of wonder, like a beautiful dream.

With twinkles like stars that softly call,
Whispers of secrets, casting a spell over all.

Her gaze is a canvas where feelings unfold,
A storm of emotions, both tender and bold.

They dance in the moonlight, a soft, sweet plea,
In the stillness of night, they speak just to me.

So charming and lovely, like dew on a flower,
Each glance is a promise, fills my heart with power.

A longing for closeness, where love takes its flight,
In the depths of her eyes, I find pure delight.

They seek a love that's gentle and true,
A craving for warmth that feels fresh and new.

In the quiet of night, they linger and sway,
Within those soft depths, I wish to stay.

Oh, how I am captivated, so swept by her grace,
In the world of her eyes, I've found my safe place.

With each treasured glance, I feel myself near,
For in her sweet gaze, my heart disappears.

12. Velvet Lips

As night falls softly, where dreams come alive,
Her lips hold a magic that pulls me inside.
Crimson and sweet, like the finest wine,
With every glance, I feel the sign.

Her top lip curls, a playful tease,
The bottom one whispers and invites with please
They draw me near with a lovely embrace
In her warmth, I find my hiding place.

Each shimmering scale tells secrets so bold,
Of passion and longing, in the night's gentle hold.
With every caress, new sparks will ignite,
As shadows dance softly in the moonlight.

Come closer, she breathes, her voice like a sigh,
Where heartbeats echo and sweet feelings fly.
In the heat of desire, our souls start to blend,
Sipping on love as the moments extend.

Let our bodies move in a sweet, perfect way,
With kisses that linger, let's savor the day.
In a dance full of love, two hearts intertwine,
On this sheet of longing, our spirits align.

13. Sacred Secrets

In ancient India's hallowed grounds we roam,
With sacred temples, where love and faith call home.
My friend, my secret love, by my side I hold,
Together we wander, our hearts beating bold.

Oh, almighty creator, we come to your sacred place,
To ask for your blessings, and a loving space.
Grant us the courage, to reveal our hearts to each other,
And let our love shine bright, like the morning after.

In this land of beauty, where temples stand tall and
proud,
We seek your permission, to love each other without a
cloud.
Let our friendship blossom, into a love so true,
And guide us on our journey, with a heart that's pure
and new.

Oh, Gods above, who witness every plea,
Hear now my prayer, for her to stay with me.

Let time stand still, and let our futures blend,
Forever bound, until the very end.

Oh, almighty creator, we thank you for this land,
Where love and faith entwine, hand in hand.
Grant us the gift of love, that we just be together,
In your sacred presence, under the Indian sun.

14. Beyond Words

Listen dear, for this truth I must share
My love for you is beyond compare
Think I'm just saying what you want to hear?
Oh yaara, you're uniquely dear

You wonder if you're just another face in the throng
But in my eyes, you stand where you belong
Ordinary compliments simply won't do
For someone as extraordinary as you

Alluring, When you're in my view
My world stops, my thoughts renew
Your touch is like a soothing balm
Bringing peace, dispelling qualm

Charming and lovable? That's just the start
You've completely captured my heart
Others may flutter by like leaves in the breeze
But you're the one who brings me ease

Beyond your beauty, which is clear to see
It's your presence and aura that's captured me
Your spirit, your soul, so pure and true
That's the foundation of my love for you

15. Unspoken Wishes

There's something special in the air,
The way you smile, the way you care.
Each time I see you passing by,
My heart can't help but softly sigh.

Your presence fills my days with light,
Makes everything feel pure and right.
I wonder if you ever see,
Just what you mean to me.

The little things you say and do,
Make me want to be with you.
Your kindness shows in all you do,
Makes me hope you're feeling too.

When our eyes meet across the room,
My heart just starts to softly bloom.
I find myself lost in your gaze,
Lost in these wonderful days.

Please tell me that I'm not alone,
That these feelings we both own.
Let's turn this dream into our start,
Two souls, one beating heart.

16. Love On Wheels

This city shines with days so bright,
With you beside me, all feels right.
We drive around in my simple car,
Just holding hands, we'll go quite far.

Our playlist playing numbers, old and new,
Your smiling eyes say "I love you."
A gentle touch, a sweet small tease,
Our hearts so happy, minds at ease.

We laugh and talk of daily things,
Your voice such joy and comfort brings.
Such sweet laughter fills the air,
A special love, beyond compare.

We stay close as time flies past,
Making memories that will last.
The city lights shine on our way,
Our bond grows stronger each passing day.

17. Wine & Cigarettes

The room was glowing with a warm subtle light,
A bedside lamp casting our shadow, a playful sight.

Our playlist played numbers we both adore,
Lost in that moment we wanted each other more.

The wine was rich, red like a sunset's kiss,
With every sip taken, we sank into bliss.

The smoke curled around us, dreams in the air,
Each puff a treasure, both light and rare.

Your eyes found mine, a spark in the night,
Lost in the music, everything felt right.

My fingers traced slowly, your skin so divine,
Wrapped in each other, we sipped on our wine.

Each touch felt like magic, a soft, sweet request,
In this quiet moment, we both felt so blessed.

The music grew louder, a wave of delight,
Together we danced, through the deep of the night.

The world faded out, just us in this space,
Bathed in the warmth of our loving embrace.

Our love was the song, and the night was our play,
Until morning arrived, to chase dreams away.

18. Essence

As dawn spills light through curtains high,
A new day's promise paints the sky.

Dear your skin, a canvas pure and bright,
Exudes notes of exotic fragrance in the night.

Salted caramel, temptation's way,
Pistachio dreams that drift and sway.

With every pulse and rhythmic beat,
Jasmine's spell makes passion sweet.

Vanilla clouds drift soft and rare,
Like silken whispers in the air.

Each note entwines like threads divine,
A scent that makes the stars align.

The room ablaze, all else now gone,
As passion carries lovers on.

A fragrant storm makes hearts race wild,
In sweet surrender, both beguiled.

19. Echoes of Us

If fate should pull our hands apart one day,
Remember love's not measured by our stay.
In secret chambers of our hearts we grew,
A love so pure that only we both knew.

Be strong, my love, if storms should cloud our way,
Though tears may fall, we knew this price to pay.
I'll keep your picture close when night grows deep,
And in my dreams, our promises I'll keep.

Move forward if the world tears us apart,
But know you'll have a chamber in my heart.
Your smile will guide me through the darkest night,
Like stars that shine though hidden from our sight.

If life demands we walk on separate roads,
Remember joy, not sorrow, that we sowed.
I'll see your face in every morning's light,
And feel your love when nothing else feels right.

Be brave enough to let our love transform,
Into a strength that helps us weather storms.
For though apart, the story will never end
Two souls forever bound, beyond just friend.

20. Invisible Threads

I promise you with all my heart,
Even when we are far apart.
Though today we hide our love,
I swear by stars that shine above.

Tomorrow when the world's at peace,
Our need to hide will finally cease.
Until that day, please wait for me,
As sure as waves roll in the sea.

I'll think of you at morning light,
And send you wishes late at night.
No matter where my path may lead,
Your love is all I'll ever need.

Though fate won't let us share our days,
We'll walk our own, separate ways.
But in my heart, you'll always be
The love that set my spirit free.

21. Graceful Goodbye

To all who loved but could not stay,
Whose hearts still beat in love's sweet way,
In busy streets and quiet rooms,
Where once their love did brightly bloom.

They kept fond thoughts like hidden gold,
In secret places, stories untold,
Yet spoke no harsh words of their pain,
And let their faith in love remain.

From north to south, from east to west,
They blessed the love that made them blessed,
Though fate had plans they could not see,
They thanked the bond that set hearts free.

And you, dear reader, I thank you too,
For all the love you've held so true,
Your gentle heart, your kindness pure,
Makes love's great beauty still endure.

www.ingramcontent.com/pod-product-compliance
Lightning Source LLC
Chambersburg PA
CBHW070611160726
48003CB00005B/2212